Original title:
The Road Forward



Author: Olivia Oja
ISBN HARDBACK: 978-9916-89-688-4
ISBN PAPERBACK: 978-9916-89-689-1
ISBN EBOOK: 978-9916-89-690-7

## Breathed into New Life

In the silence, a breath does rise,
From the depths of shadows, hope complies.
Light pierces through the darkest night,
In the stillness, we find our light.

Hearts awaken with love's embrace,
Seeing grace in every place.
New beginnings softly unfold,
In faith, we become bold.

Every moment a chance to see,
The hand of the Divine, guiding me.
Through the storm, we learn to sway,
Breathed into life, we find our way.

## Holy Whispers Guiding Us

Amidst the noise, a voice so clear,
Whispers of love, banishing fear.
In the chaos, we seek divine,
Holy guidance, forever intertwined.

Paths illuminated by sacred light,
Gently leading us through the night.
In our hearts, the truth resides,
With each step, our faith abides.

Listen closely, let stillness reign,
In every sorrow, there’s joy to gain.
Holy whispers, forever near,
In every heartbeat, the Spirit steers.

## From Despair to Devotion

In the valley of tears, despair takes hold,
Yet in the shadows, a story unfolds.
From ashes we rise, spirit renewed,
In every heartbreak, love is imbued.

Hands lifted high, we find our song,
In the depths of pain, we learn to be strong.
Devotion blossoms where hope is sown,
Through trials, our faith has grown.

Each stumble brings lessons divine,
In the chaos, His light will shine.
From despair to devotion, we tread,
On paths of grace, we are led.

## The Covenant of Change

In the stillness of dawn, a promise made,
The covenant of change, never to fade.
With every heartbeat, we embrace the flow,
Transformation waits, as we learn to grow.

Seasons shifting, the world spins bright,
In each ending, we find new light.
Trusting the journey, hand in hand,
In faith, we rise, united we stand.

Every struggle a chance to refine,
In the presence of love, our souls align.
Embrace the change, for we are reborn,
In the dawn of the day, a new morn.

## A Symphony of New Beginnings

In dawn's light, hope is reborn,
Each breath a gift, a sacred morn.
With every step, the path is clear,
A symphony of love draws near.

Faith whispers soft, in gentle breeze,
Encouraging hearts to find their ease.
Bound by grace, we rise and stand,
United in the Maker's hand.

New chapters bloom, the past released,
In quiet moments, souls find peace.
Waves of mercy wash ashore,
Each new beginning—an open door.

Together we walk, strong and true,
In every phase, His light shines through.
With open hearts, we sing our song,
In harmony, we all belong.

So let us dance in faith's embrace,
Trusting love will guide our pace.
A symphony plays, forever bright,
New beginnings bathed in holy light.

## Sanctity in Every Step

In shadows deep, our spirits soar,
Finding grace on sacred floor.
With humble hearts, we seek the way,
Sanctity in each new day.

The whispering winds, a voice so clear,
Reminding us that love draws near.
With every trial, faith is our shield,
In holy trust, our wounds are healed.

Each step we take, a prayer unfolds,
Stories of courage, forever told.
In kindness shared and compassion shown,
The seeds of hope are gently sown.

In silence found, we hear His call,
A loving presence that comforts all.
Together we journey, hand in hand,
In sacred unity, we firmly stand.

So let us walk with hearts aglow,
Embracing love in all we know.
Sanctity shines in the paths we tread,
Guided by light that's heavenly led.

## Streams of Grace Flowing Forward

In the quiet, grace does flow,
Washing hearts where shadows grow.
Tender whispers, love's embrace,
Guiding souls in sacred space.

Each step taken, faith our guide,
In the waters, we abide.
Hope awakens, fears retreat,
In His mercy, we are fleet.

To the rivers, pure and bright,
Cleansing sorrows, bringing light.
Every drop a promise made,
In the streams, our past shall fade.

As we journey, hands held high,
Faithful never shall we die.
With each wave, our burdens shed,
Following where He has led.

Grace unending, flowing strong,
In this current, we belong.
Let us trust and carry forth,
In His love, we find our worth.

## The Light of Promise Ahead

In the dawn, a light will shine,
Drawing near, the heart divine.
Every shadow fades away,
With His glory, we shall stay.

Walking paths of hope and grace,
Each new morning, seek His face.
Whispers soft, a calming breeze,
In His presence, all is ease.

Though the storms may rage and roar,
His sweet peace is evermore.
Trust the promise, hold it tight,
In the dark, He'll be our light.

Mountains high and valleys low,
In our hearts, His love will grow.
Every step in faith we take,
Brings us closer for His sake.

So we journey hand in hand,
With the Savior, strong we stand.
Light of promise leads the way,
Guiding us through each new day.

## Destined for the Infinite

In the vastness of the sky,
Dreams take flight, we rise and fly.
Heaven's call, a beckoning,
In our hearts, His love we sing.

Though the world may seem so grim,
In the light, we trust in Him.
Destinies intertwined in grace,
In His arms, we find our place.

Every heartbeat tells a tale,
Of the love that will prevail.
Boundless joy in every breath,
In His arms, there's no more death.

Journey forth, oh souls so dear,
In His promise, have no fear.
Infinite, our spirits soar,
In His glory, we explore.

Together we will rise and shine,
Guided by the hand divine.
Toward the light, our paths align,
Destined for the grand design.

## Embracing Change God's Way

In His will, we find our peace,
With each moment, doubts release.
Seasons turn, and we shall glide,
Trusting all the while in His guide.

Change arrives, a sacred gift,
In His love, our spirits lift.
Every challenge, purpose brings,
In our hearts, the Spirit sings.

Letting go of what we knew,
Embracing all that's fresh and true.
In the shift, His grace remains,
Through the trials, joy sustains.

New horizons call us near,
With the Lord, we have no fear.
In each change, His hand we see,
Crafting lives, His tapestry.

So together, hand in hand,
We shall journey to His land.
With each chapter, trust His way,
Embracing change, come what may.

## Aroma of Worship

In the stillness of dawn's embrace,
Hearts rise like incense, pure and wide.
Each whisper of prayer finds its place,
In the temple where spirits abide.

Voices blend in harmony's song,
As faith weaves through every plea.
In this moment, we all belong,
In sacred unity, we are free.

Hands lifted high, in surrendering grace,
A tapestry woven with love and trust.
In His presence, we find our space,
Transforming our hearts, as we must.

Joyful echoes fill the air,
As worship flows from each heart's core.
Lost in reverence, we lay bare,
In the aroma of worship, we soar.

With each breath, a promise we keep,
In sacred rhythm, souls entwined.
Through all the valleys and the steep,
In worship, our hope is defined.

## Treasures along the Trail

Along the path where footsteps tread,
Golden lessons await the way.
With every prayer that's gently said,
Treasures unfold with light of day.

The trials faced become our guide,
Gifts wrapped in faith through every test.
In the shadows, love doth bide,
Within the heart, we find our rest.

As we wander, hands held tight,
Grace ignites the journey made.
With weary hearts, we find the light,
In every moment, love displayed.

Mountains high and valleys low,
Each step reveals, a truth set free.
In seeking wisdom, we come to know,
All riches found in humility.

So take these treasures, deep inside,
For faith's gentle path shall not fail.
In every joy and sorrow's tide,
The spirit guides us along the trail.

## Sanctuary of the Soul

Within the hush of twilight's glow,
The sacred heart begins to breathe.
In quietude, our spirits flow,
Transforming pain, we take our leave.

A wooden chair, a place to rest,
Where solitude and love collide.
In the stillness, we feel blessed,
In the haven where faith can guide.

Songs of angels fill the air,
While shadows dance upon the wall.
In this space, we lay our care,
A tender whisper, love's sweet call.

Each moment shared in divine embrace,
Wraps around us, a gentle balm.
In the sanctuary, we find grace,
Resting in the spirit's calm.

Here in silence, our hearts align,
Steeped in mercy, we shall rise.
This sanctuary, forever mine,
A refuge found beneath the skies.

## Starry Pilgrimage

Underneath a canvas dark and vast,
We journey forth with hearts alight.
Stars above, our calls are cast,
Guiding pilgrims through the night.

With each step on this hallowed ground,
We seek the truth in silence deep.
In the chaos, peace is found,
As the heavens watch and keep.

Every star, a tale untold,
Whispers of grace, woven in time.
In their glow, our spirits behold,
A path adorned with endless rhyme.

The night sky, a symphony, grand,
As we journey 'neath the sacred dome.
Every footprint, a prayer, a hand,
Welcoming us closer to Home.

So onward we tread, with faith sincere,
On this pilgrimage through the dark.
In the starry embrace, we conquer fear,
Igniting hope, a vibrant spark.

## Pilgrimage of the Soul

In shadows long, the soul does roam,
Through valleys deep, away from home.
Each step a prayer, a silent plea,
To find the light, to set it free.

With every dawn, the spirit wakes,
The path unfolds, the earth it shakes.
In stillness found, and whispers heard,
The heartbeats echo, a holy word.

Mountains rise with sacred grace,
Each summit reaches a holy place.
The journey calls, the stars align,
In faith we walk, the path divine.

Through storms that rage and winds that howl,
We find our way, the sacred bowl.
Embraced in light, the shadows fade,
In love and hope, our fears are laid.

So onward now, the way unfolds,
Each step a story, wisdom told.
A pilgrimage of heart and mind,
In every soul, the truth we find.

## Whispers of the Celestial Way

In twilight's breath, the stars do sing,
A melody of the ethereal spring.
Each note a whisper, soft and clear,
Guiding the hearts that draw near.

The moonlight dances on trembling leaves,
Awakening souls, and healing grieves.
With each sigh, the heavens speak,
In sacred hush, the weak grow strong.

A tapestry woven of light and grace,
In every thread, the divine face.
The cosmic chords, they intertwine,
In unity found, the soul aligns.

So let us walk in the starry night,
With open hearts, embracing the light.
Together we'll journey, hand in hand,
Through whispers soft, the truth of the land.

With every step, the spirit glows,
In sacred dance, the river flows.
In prophecy, our hearts obey,
The whispers guide us along the way.

## Ascending through the Veil

A curtain drawn, the veil between,
In twilight hours, a sacred scene.
We seek the light, the truth revealed,
In sacred space, our fates are sealed.

Each breath a step, a gentle rise,
Through realms unseen, beyond the skies.
In stillness found, the spirit breaks,
Through every fear, a journey takes.

The wandering light, it calls our name,
To venture forth, to seek the flame.
In sacred trust, we face the dawn,
A new horizon, a spirit drawn.

With wings of faith, we claim our flight,
Ascend we toward the endless light.
In unity and grace, we soar,
Through every veil, forevermore.

Our souls entwined, the journey's grace,
In love and peace, we find our place.
Together we rise, we are whole,
Ascending ever, the sacred soul.

## Temples of Tomorrow

In hearts of stone, the spirits dwell,
A timeless echo, a sacred well.
In every prayer, a future brims,
Within these walls, our hope begins.

The foundations laid in love's embrace,
A temple built, a holy space.
With every stone, a dream takes flight,
In whispered prayers, we find our light.

We gather here, in faith we stand,
Hand in hand, a united band.
Through trials faced and battles won,
The dawn of peace, it has begun.

The roof above, a canvas wide,
Where stars collide, and shadows hide.
With every heart, a story told,
In temples bright, our love unfolds.

So let us raise our voices high,
In unity beneath the sky.
For in our dreams, tomorrow waits,
In temples forged, our hearts create.

## The Eternal Dance of Destiny

In shadows cast by fate's own hand,
We twirl upon this sacred land.
Each step a whisper, each glance a prayer,
Entwined in grace, a love affair.

The stars above in rhythm guide,
Their wisdom flows like a gentle tide.
With every heartbeat, truths unfold,
In unity, our spirits bold.

The sun will rise, the night will fall,
Yet in this dance, we hear the call.
For destiny's road is paved with light,
A symphony of day and night.

Let anguish fade, let joy arise,
In this eternal dance, we rise.
With every turn, we find our way,
In faith and hope, we softly sway.

Together we move, together we sing,
In the harmony, the angels bring.
Destiny's dance, forever blessed,
In divine embrace, we find our rest.

## Manifesto of the Spirit's Journey

With every heartbeat, a tale unfolds,
In depths of silence, the spirit holds.
A journey vast, through time and space,
In search of wisdom, in search of grace.

Guided by stars, we wander free,
Navigating realms of eternity.
Each challenge met, each lesson learned,
In the flame of truth, our souls are burned.

From dawn to dusk, through shadow's veil,
We speak our truth, we tell our tale.
In the stillness, we find our core,
A manifesto of forevermore.

Embrace the winds that shift and sway,
For each step forward, we find our way.
In unity's song, our spirits soar,
A journey sacred, forevermore.

Let love be our compass, strong and true,
In every moment, in all we do.
With open hearts and steadfast minds,
The spirit journeys, and joy it finds.

## The Garden of Tomorrow's Dreams

In the garden where hopes take flight,
Dreams blossom ‘neath the soft moonlight.
Each petal whispers of futures unfurled,
In sacred soil, a new dawn is swirled.

The seeds of faith, in hearts entwined,
Nurtured by love, by grace aligned.
Through trials faced, in shadows cast,
We gather strength, our roots hold fast.

A tapestry woven with colors bold,
Stories of courage and beauty told.
With every bloom, a promise we keep,
In this garden, our souls will leap.

Let the rain fall, let the sun shine bright,
In the garden of dreams, all spirits ignite.
With every harvest, new hope we find,
In unity’s embrace, in love intertwined.

From the earth, we gather, from the sky,
A future crafted, where spirits fly.
With faith as our guide, we rise and we weave,
In the garden of tomorrow, we dare to believe.

## Celestial Guiding Lights

In the quiet of the night, they gleam,
Celestial beings, guiding each dream.
With wisdom ancient, love pure and bright,
They dance among the stars, in soft delight.

Each flicker speaks of journeys afar,
In their embrace, we're never ajar.
Through trials of earth, they hold our hand,
With spirits lifted, we boldly stand.

With every wish cast upon the skies,
A testament to the heart that flies.
Their light reminds us, we are not alone,
In the tapestry of life, we are sewn.

Let courage bloom, let hearts ignite,
With celestial lights to lead the fight.
In the embrace of the cosmic dance,
We rise and shine, we take a chance.

With every dawn, their whispers hear,
A song of love that draws us near.
In the cosmos vast, our purpose bright,
We journey together, in eternal light.

## Priestly Voices in the Wilderness

In silence they wander, the wise and the meek,
Whispers of faith in the stillness they seek.
With shadows that dance on the paths they tread,
They carry the light where the lost are led.

Beneath the vast heavens, where spirits reside,
They call forth the heavens to walk by their side.
Through trials of fire and rivers of gray,
The echoes of love guide them day by day.

With hands raised in blessing, they breathe out the grace,
In rapture, they find every moment's embrace.
Through valleys and storms, their weary hearts sing,
In unity found, they discover their king.

The sacred words spoken, like seeds in the earth,
They nurture the weary, renewing their birth.
In the heart of the wilderness, trials refined,
Priestly voices uplift, embrace the entwined.

## The Voyage of the Soul's Desires

Across the vast ocean of dreams and of prayers,
The soul takes its voyage, surrendering cares.
With stars as their compass, they sail through the night,
Guided by visions, divine and bright.

In whispers of longing, the heart learns to yearn,
Each wave holds a promise, a lesson to learn.
With sails made of hope and the winds of desire,
They journey toward truth, their spirits aspire.

From shores of temptation to islands of grace,
They seek what is holy, a sacred embrace.
In storms of confusion, they anchor in faith,
While light from above grants them courage and faith.

As dawn greets the ocean, horizons unfold,
The stories and struggles, in silence retold.
The voyage of souls, in timeless pursuit,
Finds strength in connection, a bond absolute.

## Sacred Pilgrims of the New Dawn

With footsteps in rhythm, they rise with the sun,
Sacred pilgrims traveling, their journey begun.
Through valleys of sorrow and mountains of praise,
In search of the light, they traverse ancient ways.

Their hearts beat like drums to the sacred refrain,
In unity moving, they dance through the rain.
With offerings cherished, they share and they sing,
Of hope and of love, the gifts they can bring.

Through deserts of longing and rivers of tears,
They nourish their spirits, they conquer their fears.
Each step is a blessing, each breath a new chance,
In the tapestry woven, their souls find romance.

As dawn paints the sky in a brilliant array,
They carry the light into each brand new day.
With faith as their compass, their voices entwined,
Sacred pilgrims gather, their destinies aligned.

## Vows of Resilience and Hope

In shadows of doubt, they gather as one,
A chorus of strength, their journey begun.
With vows of resilience, they rise from the fall,
In unity standing, they answer the call.

With hands joined together, they weather the storm,
In love's gentle shelter, they find a new form.
Each promise a beacon, a light in the night,
Transforming the darkness, igniting the light.

For every sorrow they carry, they weave,
Threads of compassion, for they shall believe.
In harmony's music, they craft their true fate,
With patience and courage, their spirits await.

Through struggles and trials, they flourish and grow,
With hearts full of wisdom, their truths brightly glow.
Vows of resilience, like seeds gently sown,
In gardens of hope, their legacy grown.

## Celestial Adventures Awaiting

In the stillness of the night, I seek,
Stars above, their wisdom they speak.
Wings of faith carry me high,
To realms where the spirit can fly.

Guided by the moon's soft glow,
Paths unfold, where angels bestow.
Each step a dance in divine grace,
In the universe's warm embrace.

Through cosmic dreams, my heart will soar,
To sacred lands where souls explore.
Every secret of the skies,
Awaits the heart that seeks and tries.

Voices of the ancients call,
In the silence, I hear it all.
Echoes of love fill the air,
Reminding me of the light I share.

In celestial adventures vast and grand,
I journey forth, by the spirit's hand.
With every dawn, new wonders await,
In a tapestry divine, I await my fate.

## The Light of Hope's Embrace

Amidst the storms that dark clouds bring,
A flicker glows, a gentle wing.
Hope whispers softly, do not fear,
For love's embrace is ever near.

In the silence, a prayer takes flight,
Carried aloft by the stars so bright.
Each breath a testament of grace,
In the warmth of hope's sweet embrace.

When shadows dance, and doubts arise,
Look to the heavens, the eternal skies.
With every tear, a seed is sown,
In the garden of faith, we are never alone.

The dawn will break, and light will stream,
Illuminating paths, like a waking dream.
In the strength of love, we find our way,
Through the trials of night into the day.

Rejoice, for every heart must find,
The light of hope that binds mankind.
In unity, we'll rise and soar,
Together in love, forevermore.

## Celestial Horizons Beckon

Across the sky's vast, infinite sea,
Celestial horizons beckon to me.
Amidst the stars, my spirit yearns,
To unravel the mystery, the heart learns.

In the twilight glow where dreams take flight,
Guided by faith through the velvet night.
Each heartbeat echoes in the cosmic choir,
Awakening the soul's eternal fire.

The universe speaks in a whispering breeze,
In every rustle of the ancient trees.
As I gaze upon the celestial spin,
The journey starts where creation begins.

With open arms, I embrace the unknown,
Trusting the path that leads me home.
In the depths of the night, a guiding spark,
Illuminates the way within the dark.

The call of the heavens stirs my core,
Inviting me to explore evermore.
In every star lies a story untold,
A promise of love, both tender and bold.

## Balancing Between Shadows and Luminescence

In the dance of light, shadows play,
I walk a path both bright and gray.
Between the dark and the radiant beam,
I find my faith, I find my dream.

The flicker of hope ignites the night,
Guiding my heart to embrace the light.
For in every shadow that we face,
Lies the chance for love's warm embrace.

With each step taken along this way,
I learn to cherish both night and day.
In the balance, my spirit grows,
Through trials faced, true strength flows.

The whispers of wisdom fill the air,
Inviting me to reflect and care.
In the dance of shadows, I find my song,
A melody where all souls belong.

Embracing both the light and shade,
In every moment, love is conveyed.
As I walk this line of divine design,
I see the beauty in the intertwine.

So I hold each paradox with grace,
In the tapestry of time and space.
For in this balance, a truth is clear,
That love transcends both hope and fear.

## Chronicles of the Faithful

In shadows deep, our spirits yearn,
With every prayer, the candles burn.
Through trials faced, we stand as one,
In faith's embrace, our hearts have won.

The sacred texts, our guiding light,
Reveal the path through darkest night.
With voices raised in harmony,
We find our strength in unity.

From mountains high to valleys low,
The grace of love begins to flow.
Each story told, a life reborn,
In every heart, the hope is sworn.

From dusk till dawn, in silence pray,
For peace to guide us on our way.
With every breath, we seek the truth,
In tales of old, we find our youth.

As stars align in skies above,
We journey forth, embraced by love.
Chronicles of the faithful sing,
Of every soul, the joy they bring.

## Veils of the Unknown

Behind the veils, the whispers call,
A sacred dance that unites us all.
In mysteries wrapped, we seek to know,
The heart of God, in ebb and flow.

With every question, a seed is sown,
In quietude, the truth is grown.
Through shadows cast, the light will shine,
In every soul, the divine design.

Veils of the unknown gently part,
Revealing love that fills the heart.
In every sigh, a prayer ascends,
As boundless grace defines our ends.

In sacred stillness, we shall find,
The echoes of the ancient mind.
With open hearts, we shall embrace,
The gentle touch of Heaven's grace.

So let us walk through veils unseen,
In faith we gather, in hope we glean.
For in the unknown, we are made whole,
In every journey, we find our soul.

## Embracing the Sacred Unknown

In sacred realms where shadows play,
We find the light that shows the way.
Each moment's breath, a gift divine,
In every heartbeat, love will shine.

To embrace the unknown is to believe,
In the promise of grace that we receive.
Through paths of trust, we rise and soar,
With open arms, we seek for more.

In quiet whispers, the spirit moves,
Through every trial, the heart improves.
We find our strength in sacred song,
In unity, where we belong.

The tapestry of life's design,
Weaves threads of joy and love divine.
Embracing all that life bestows,
In sacred trust, our spirit grows.

Let not the fear of what may be,
Deter our steps on this journey free.
For in the unknown, we find the light,
Embracing all, we rise to flight.

## Boundless Horizons of Devotion

On boundless skies, our hearts take flight,
In devotion pure, we seek the light.
Each sunrise brings a brand new chance,
To share our love in Heaven's dance.

With every prayer, horizons grow,
In acts of kindness, grace we sow.
Devotion strong, like rivers flow,
A sacred bond, forever glow.

Through trials faced, we gather near,
In unity, we cast out fear.
With open eyes, we choose to see,
The beauty in humanity.

Through valleys deep and mountains grand,
We walk together, hand in hand.
Each step we take, a hymn of grace,
In devotion's name, our souls embrace.

Boundless horizons, love prevails,
In faith we trust, as spirit sails.
Together we rise, forever strong,
In devotion's arms, we all belong.

## Horizon of Hope

At dawn’s first light we rise,
With hearts aflame and spirits high.
Each whisper from the skies,
Guides us forth, our souls to fly.

Through valleys low and mountains steep,
Your promise, Lord, we hold so dear.
In shadows cast, our faith won’t seep,
With every step, we draw you near.

The sun it shines on paths unknown,
Yet we find peace in your embrace.
In trials faced, we’re not alone,
For in our hearts, we find your grace.

A gentle breeze that cools the air,
Reminds us of your boundless love.
In every moment, every prayer,
We seek the light from up above.

The horizon glows with every dawn,
A beacon bright, a guiding star.
With courage strong, we journey on,
United, we shall go so far.

## Celestial Highway

On this celestial highway wide,
We travel forth with spirits free.
With every step, you are our guide,
In faith, we find our destiny.

The stars above, they shine so bright,
Illuminating paths of gold.
In darkest hours, you are the light,
A promise true, a tale retold.

Through storms that roar and winds that howl,
Your presence calms the raging sea.
In quiet moments, hear us howl,
With grateful hearts, we worship thee.

Each mile we walk, we dream of grace,
In every trial, strength we gain.
The love you share, we now embrace,
Through joy and sorrow, loss and gain.

Upon this road, we lift our song,
In harmony, our voices blend.
For in your arms, we all belong,
Our journey blessed, we shall transcend.

## Reverence in the Wilderness

In wilderness where silence reigns,
Amidst the trees, we seek and find.
Your majesty in nature's veins,
A sacred pause to still the mind.

The mountains rise, their peaks so grand,
They touch the heavens with their grace.
With open hearts, we make our stand,
In awe of you, we find our place.

The rivers flow, a gentle hymn,
With every drop, we sing your praise.
In every shadow, light within,
Your spirit moves in wondrous ways.

Through rustling leaves and whispers low,
Your presence felt, a holy breath.
In nature's beauty, love will grow,
Through every life, even in death.

With reverence, we bow in prayer,
In wilderness, our hearts align.
For in this space, we find you there,
Forever yours, our souls entwine.

## Ascending Towards Grace

As we ascend on paths divine,
With every step, we draw so near.
In you, O Lord, our hearts entwine,
Embracing truth, dispelling fear.

The clouds may rise and shadows fall,
But we, in faith, shall hold our ground.
Your love, it echoes through us all,
A symphony of joys profound.

In gentle breezes come the signs,
That guide us onward, day by day.
In trials faced, your light defines,
The path we tread, the love we pray.

With eyes to heaven, hands held high,
We journey forth, one soul, one grace.
Each moment lived, we will not sigh,
For in your arms, we find our place.

As we ascend towards the skies,
We trust in you, our hearts aglow.
With every breath, our spirits rise,
Together, Lord, through ebb and flow.

## Pathways of Faith

In shadows deep, the light breaks through,
A whisper soft, the heart renews.
Each step we take, on sacred ground,
In faith we rise, in grace we're found.

The stars above, they guide our way,
Through trials fierce, we learn to pray.
With open hearts, we seek the truth,
In every moment, a chance for youth.

The dawn will come, with promise bright,
Our souls aflame, we chase the light.
With every breath, we seek His face,
On pathways worn, we find our place.

As rivers flow, our spirits soar,
In unity, we long for more.
The higher call, it stirs within,
A journey brave, where love begins.

Together bound, we walk in grace,
No fear can hold, in His embrace.
Through every storm, we stand as one,
In faith and love, our race is run.

## Steps Towards the Divine

In quiet morn, we turn to prayer,
A moment still, our burdens bare.
With lifting hearts, we greet the day,
In searching souls, the light will stay.

Each step we take, a dance of hope,
In sacred trust, we learn to cope.
With eyes lifted, we seek the sky,
In faith we dare, our spirits fly.

The path is long, yet never bleak,
In whispered love, His voices speak.
With open hands, our offerings shared,
In humble service, we show we cared.

As seasons change, so do we grow,
In trials faced, His mercies flow.
Together bold, we walk this road,
With hearts ignited, we share the load.

In every joy, in every tear,
His presence felt, our vision clear.
With every heartbeat, we aspire,
To know the One who lights the fire.

## Journey of the Spirit

On this vast road, our spirits roam,
In search of peace, we find our home.
With gentle steps, we journey on,
In every dusk, there shines a dawn.

Through valleys low, and mountains high,
With faith as wings, we learn to fly.
In sacred moments, we are whole,
The path unfolds, revealing soul.

Through ancient woods, the silence sings,
In every breath, new life it brings.
With every pause, His love ignites,
On journey long, we seek His sights.

Across the seas, and through the night,
We gather strength, in shared delight.
With open hearts, we seek His grace,
In every trial, we find our place.

Together we tread, through joy and strife,
In this great tapestry, we weave our life.
In love's embrace, we find our way,
To journey forth, come what may.

## Pilgrimage of the Heart

In every step, a prayer is sown,
In quiet places, we're not alone.
With hearts aflame, we seek the light,
On pilgrimage, both day and night.

Through ancient lands, the spirits call,
In every shadow, we find our all.
With faith as our guide, we cannot stray,
In love's embrace, we make our way.

The road may twist, the path may bend,
Yet in His arms, we find our friend.
With every hill, and every fall,
We rise again, we answer the call.

With every song, pure joy does spring,
In harmony, we lift our offering.
Together bound, through thick and thin,
In pilgrimage, new life begins.

In every heart, the spark does shine,
With open souls, we seek the divine.
Through trials faced, we persevere,
In pilgrimage, we draw Him near.

## The Light Ahead

In shadows deep, we seek the flame,
A guiding star, in His holy name.
Through trials faced, our spirits soar,
In faith we find, forevermore.

With every step, the path unveiled,
His love our guide, we shall not fail.
In moments dark, His grace ignites,
The light ahead, our hearts' delights.

Through storms we walk, hand in hand,
His promises firm like golden sand.
In whispers soft, His voice we hear,
Leading us forth, erasing fear.

In prayer we rise, to heights divine,
Our souls entwined, a sacred line.
With humble hearts, we lift His praise,
In endless love, our spirits blaze.

The light ahead, our beacon bright,
Illuminates the darkest night.
With faith as compass, we shall tread,
Towards the promise, the light ahead.

**Transcendence in Motion**

In stillness found, the heart takes flight,
Beyond the veils of earthly sight.
With open arms, we welcome grace,
A dance of souls, in sacred space.

Through trials faced, we learn to rise,
With every step, our spirits wise.
In moments lost, we find the way,
Transcendence blooms with every prayer.

With each breath drawn, the world dissolves,
In harmony, our hearts evolve.
We journey forth, side by side,
In faith eternal, our guides abide.

Through hills and valleys, light will shine,
In unity, we intertwine.
With love, we break the chains of fears,
In sacred music, dispelling tears.

Transcendence reached, in every beat,
A rhythm sweet, where souls meet.
In every moment, divinely spun,
Together as one, our journey begun.

## Echoes of Eternity

In whispers soft, the past resounds,
Through sacred halls, where love abounds.
Each echo tells of faith's embrace,
Of timeless truth, a boundless grace.

In every heart, a story weaves,
Of hope reborn, as spirit believes.
The moments lived, forever stay,
As echoes guide us on our way.

With every prayer, the voices rise,
In unity, our faith supplies.
Transcending time, inseparable thread,
In echoes of eternity, we’re led.

Through trials faced, our strength is known,
In love's embrace, we're never alone.
The journey vast, our spirits soar,
In echoes heard, forevermore.

With hearts aligned, we walk as one,
In sacred light, a new day’s begun.
Each echo heard, a guiding song,
In eternity’s arms, we all belong.

## Sacred Ascent

With every dawn, the spirit wakes,
A journey starts, as hearts embrace.
Through valleys low and mountains steep,
In sacred ascent, our promises keep.

Climbing high, we seek the light,
In faith we rise, dispelling night.
Through trials faced, our souls ignite,
In love's embrace, our hearts take flight.

Each step we take, a prayer in motion,
A river flows, an endless ocean.
With every breath, our dreams align,
In sacred ascent, His will divine.

With every trial, our spirits grow,
In unity, we'll ever sow.
The path ahead, a holy quest,
In sacred ascent, we find our rest.

As we ascend, we sing His praise,
In every heartbeat, His love displays.
With eyes on Him, our journey clear,
In sacred ascent, we have no fear.

## Seeking the Blessed Way

In shadows deep, where spirits tread,
The heart will search, where grace is led.
With whispers soft, the soul will sway,
In humble prayer, I seek the way.

The light shall guide, through trials vast,
I lay my burdens, forget the past.
In faith's embrace, the journey starts,
With every step, O Lord, my heart.

Through valleys low, and mountains high,
Your love will hold, I will not cry.
In every tear, a lesson learned,
Towards the truth, my spirit yearned.

In sacred hymns, our voices blend,
To seek the blessed, until the end.
In unity, we find our song,
To walk the path, where we belong.

With every dawn, a chance to rise,
To spread my wings and touch the skies.
In holy peace, my trust I'll lay,
Forever sought, the blessed way.

## Beneath the Everlasting Sky

Beneath the sky, so vast and wide,
I feel Your presence, by my side.
With every star, a wish I cast,
In faith's embrace, the shadows passed.

The morning sun, a golden ray,
Illuminates the path I lay.
In nature's song, I hear the call,
Your love, dear Lord, it binds us all.

With gentle winds that kiss my face,
I find in stillness, sacred space.
In every breath, a prayer I send,
Beneath the sky, I know You mend.

Through storms that rage, and nights so long,
With quiet hope, I stand still strong.
For in the trials, You are near,
A guiding light, forever clear.

In fields of green, and waters pure,
Your love surrounds, my heart is sure.
Beneath the sky, I feel Your might,
In every journey, You are my light.

## Callings from the Beyond

From ancient times, the voices rise,
Whispers of wisdom from the skies.
With every moment, heed the call,
In silence deep, we hear it all.

In sacred texts, the truths unfold,
Stories of faith, the brave and bold.
Each tale a beacon, shining bright,
Guiding us through the darkest night.

The echoes ring of souls once near,
Calling us forth, to persevere.
In hearts devoted, love does shine,
In every act, a touch divine.

With open hearts, we seek the way,
To follow paths where spirits play.
In unity, we lift our hands,
To share the love that understanding spans.

From mountains high to valleys low,
The call resounds, in high and low.
With faith unwavering, we press on,
To honor those who've come and gone.

## Chasing Divine Echoes

In quiet moments, I hear the sound,
Of sacred echoes, all around.
The heart attuned, to whispers divine,
In every heartbeat, love does shine.

Through fragrant blooms, and rivers wide,
I chase the truths that dwell inside.
In gentle waves, the spirit flows,
In sacred places, the knowing grows.

With every breath, I seek Your grace,
In all of nature, I find my place.
Through trials faced, in joy or pain,
The echoes linger, love's sweet refrain.

We are the branches, ever entwined,
Rooted in faith, the heart aligned.
With every prayer, we lift our voice,
In chasing echoes, we make our choice.

In every child, in every tear,
The essence of love, forever near.
Chasing echoes, I find my way,
In every moment, blessed today.

## Steps Beyond the Horizon

In the silence of dawn's embrace,
We seek the path of grace.
Footsteps soft on sacred ground,
In whispers of hope, we're found.

Each summit calls with a gentle sigh,
Reaching upward, we aim to fly.
With faith as our guiding light,
We journey forth through day and night.

Mountains rise like ancient spires,
Filling our souls with divine fires.
As we traverse the endless skies,
Our spirits dance where freedom lies.

Through valleys deep and rivers wide,
In every creed, we do abide.
Hand in hand, we walk this road,
Together we share love's true code.

With every step, we find our song,
In heartbeats where we all belong.
All paths converge in sacred ties,
As we step beyond the horizon's rise.

## Sacred Trails of Discovery

In the forest where shadows play,
We wander lost in prayerful sway.
Every leaf tells a story old,
Of dreams and truths, in silence bold.

Along the streams and winding ways,
The spirit whispers, gently stays.
With open hearts, we dare to seek,
The sacred trails where the humble speak.

Beneath the stars, in midnight's glow,
In every heartbeat, love will flow.
The night conceals our patterned quest,
And leads us to a heavenly rest.

As dawn approaches, light shall rise,
Revealing wonders in the skies.
We find our truth as we ascend,
On sacred trails, we will depend.

Through trials faced and fears embraced,
With every step, our souls are graced.
Together bound by hopes we share,
In sacred trails, we find our prayer.

## Illumination in the Wilderness

In the depths of the wilderness wide,
A flicker of light as our guide.
Every shadow holds a grace,
In this vast and holy space.

Among the trees, where silence reigns,
The Spirit moves through joy and pains.
We lift our eyes to the breaking dawn,
With hearts renewed, we journey on.

From mountain peaks to valleys low,
The light of faith begins to show.
Each step forward, a promise made,
In illumination, our fears will fade.

With open minds and voices clear,
We share the truth, release our fear.
In every moment, love's pure call,
In the wilderness, we rise, we fall.

As stars align to light our path,
We seek the love that conquers wrath.
Guided by hope in this vast land,
Illumination at heart's command.

## Divine Compass of the Heart

In the quietude of dawn's first light,
We turn our hearts toward the right.
With whispered grace, we take a stand,
Led by a compass, gentle hand.

Every choice, a sacred thread,
We weave our dreams with truths we've said.
A journey marked by love divine,
In every heartbeat, wisdom shines.

Through storms we brave and trials face,
In faith's embrace, we find our place.
Together walking, side by side,
Our spirits soar, our souls abide.

With every breath, the light reveals,
A world of love that gently heals.
Our inner compass leads us home,
In unity, we’re never alone.

With open arms, we greet the day,
Divine guidance shows the way.
Each step we take, a hallowed start,
As we follow the compass of the heart.

## A Prayer for New Horizons

With hearts uplifted, we seek the dawn,
A whisper of hope in a world reborn.
Guide our steps through valleys deep,
As we sow the seeds of faith and keep.

In shadows cast by doubt's cruel hand,
We search for strength to understand.
Each journey taken, a lesson learned,
A fire of wisdom forever burned.

O Lord, grant us courage to embrace the change,
To find new paths, though they may feel strange.
In every challenge, Your love will shine,
A beacon of grace, a sacred sign.

So let us rise, with spirits bold,
In unity, our stories unfold.
Hand in hand, we tread this way,
Trusting in You, come what may.

Through trials faced and blessings shared,
In grateful hearts, Your presence bared.
We lift our voices, a joyful song,
In New Horizons, where we belong.

## Embracing the Light Within

In silent prayer, the heart reflects,
A flicker of light our spirit connects.
With trust in the journey, we shall find,
The sacred truth that guides mankind.

Beneath the surface, the light does glow,
Illuminating paths we seldom know.
With each breath taken, let love reside,
Embracing the warmth that can't be denied.

In moments of doubt, feel the embrace,
A gentle reminder of divine grace.
As shadows whisper, let courage rise,
Transforming fear into hopeful skies.

With open hearts, we seek to share,
The light within us, eternally rare.
For in the depths, our True Self gleams,
A vessel of love, alive with dreams.

Together we stand, united in might,
Embracing the gift of our inner light.
With joy overflowing, our spirits soar,
In solidarity, forevermore.

## Transitions of the Heart

As seasons shift, so do our hearts,
In each departure, a new journey starts.
With faith as our anchor, we gracefully move,
Through the tapestry of life, we improve.

In moments of change, let love be the guide,
For in each ending, something new does reside.
Embracing the flow, we lift our gaze,
Trusting the process, in all of its ways.

The heart beats softly, in rhythm divine,
With every pulse, a chance to align.
So let the transitions be seen as blessings,
In every wound, a new heart's dressing.

From sorrow to joy, the dance is profound,
In learning to trust, our strength is found.
With each farewell, a door swings wide,
Inviting new journeys, where hope will abide.

Let gratitude flow in the moments now lost,
For every joy shared, we've paid the cost.
In transitions of heart, we rise and we fall,
Together in unity, we answer the call.

## Pilgrims on Sacred Soil

With faith as our compass, we traverse the land,
Pilgrims united, together we stand.
On sacred soil, where the ancients tread,
We seek the wisdom of those who've led.

Each step is a prayer, each breath a song,
In the rhythm of life, where we all belong.
Through trials and triumphs, we learn to see,
The beauty of grace that sets us free.

In humble surrender, we open our hearts,
Embracing the journey, where spirit imparts.
From mountains to valleys, our prayers arise,
A tapestry woven of hope and sighs.

As we walk this path, may love be our guide,
In every encounter, with arms open wide.
For pilgrims we are, seeking the divine,
In the footprints of faith, our lives intertwine.

So let us rejoice in the grace we receive,
In sacred gatherings, where souls believe.
For on this journey, together we toil,
As pilgrims in faith on this sacred soil.

## In the Light of New Beginnings

In dawn's embrace, we rise anew,
With hearts alight, a vision true.
Each step a prayer, each breath a song,
In sacred trust, we will belong.

The whispers of faith, gentle and clear,
Guide us through trials, calming our fear.
In every moment, His love we seek,
A promise of strength for the weary and weak.

The sun breaks forth, a radiant sign,
Illuminating paths that brightly align.
With hope like a flame, let us ignite,
The courage to walk in His guiding light.

Together we journey, hand in hand,
Embracing the grace in a sacred land.
For in forgiveness, we find our way,
In the light of new beginnings, we pray.

So let us rejoice in the gift of this day,
With hearts united, our fears held at bay.
In the light of His love, we take our stance,
With faith as our guide, we enter the dance.

## Sanctuaries of Hope and Grace

In quiet corners, where shadows fade,
We find the places where dreams are laid.
With open hearts, we gather near,
In sanctuaries of grace, freed from fear.

A gentle whisper, a soothing balm,
Brings forth the peace, a sacred calm.
Here, prayers arise like fragrant vines,
Intertwined with love, where faith enshrines.

Among the faithful, we share our plight,
Holding each other in the divine light.
In every tear, a story told,
Sanctuaries of hope, where souls are bold.

Through trials faced, we lift our voice,
In unity, we find our choice.
To rise together, strong and true,
In His presence, we are born anew.

So let us cherish these hallowed spaces,
Embrace the warmth of familiar faces.
For in the love that we freely share,
We find our blessings, a bond laid bare.

## The Chosen Path of Purpose

On winding roads where shadows play,
We seek the truth to light our way.
A call to serve, a heart inspired,
The chosen path, our spirits wired.

With each small step, we hear the call,
In the stillness, we won't fall.
For every stumble, He lifts us high,
Guided by love, we reach for the sky.

Voices echo through valleys wide,
Carrying dreams that will not hide.
Together we forge a brighter dawn,
With faith our lantern, we journey on.

In every act of kindness shown,
The seeds of purpose are deeply sown.
With open minds and willing hands,
We walk the path where His mercy stands.

So let us honor the call divine,
Embrace the journey, His love entwined.
For on this road, we shall persevere,
The chosen path, where hearts draw near.

## Following the Star of Promise

A radiant star in the midnight sky,
Guides us onward, our spirits fly.
With eyes uplifted and hearts aglow,
We follow the light wherever it goes.

In darkness deep, it shines so bright,
Leading us closer to hope and light.
With faith as our compass, we shall not stray,
Following the star shows us the way.

Each step we take, with courage entwined,
We touch the divine, our hearts aligned.
As branches of love in His vineyard grow,
Following the star, our blessings flow.

In every challenge, a lesson learned,
Through trials faced, our spirits burned.
With His guiding hand, we shall endure,
Following the star, our path is sure.

So let us gather and raise our song,
In unity, we will grow strong.
For with each heartbeat, we find our role,
Following the star, we become whole.

## The Promise Beyond

In dawn's first light, hope is born anew,
A whisper of grace, deep as the blue.
Trust in the path that leads to the skies,
For every tear, a soul surely pries.

In valleys low, the heart learns to sing,
Each sorrow a lesson that joys will bring.
God's hand does guide through the shadowed vale,
With faith as the beacon, we shall not fail.

The mountains rise, yet we climb with might,
In storms we stand, held fast by His light.
Each promise spoken, a star in the night,
Leading our spirits to futures bright.

Upon the altar of trust, we lay,
Our dreams, our fears, in love's gentle sway.
In stillness, we find the strength to proceed,
For every promise plants a sacred seed.

Upon this journey, the wise often tread,
With prayer as their compass, their worries shed.
Eternal the promise, steadfast and clear,
Together we walk, undaunted by fear.

## Serenity in Transition

In seasons that change, let go and receive,
With each falling leaf, new blessings believe.
The sacred rhythm of life ebbs and flows,
In transitions divine, the spirit grows.

Embrace the silence, the whispers of peace,
In moments of stillness, the heart finds release.
Clouds may obscure the bright sun above,
Yet deep in the storm, we gather His love.

Horizon unfolds as the dawn greets the day,
Each shadow a teacher, in a wondrous way.
When paths seem uncertain, trust leads the dance,
In faith's gentle arms, we find our romance.

With courage anew, we step into grace,
Each heartbeat a prayer in time’s warm embrace.
Through valleys of doubt and mountains of pain,
The spirit ignites, in joy, we're regained.

So cherish the moments, the ebb and the flow,
In the garden of life, let your heart sow.
For every transition, a gift we will find,
In serenity’s arms, may we all be aligned.

## Conduit of Blessings

In the quiet dawn, blessings take flight,
Like whispers of angels, wrapped in the light.
Each prayer we send, like a seed in the ground,
A conduit of love, in our hearts profound.

Through trials we face, the grace turns the tide,
Within every challenge, His hand is our guide.
With faith as our armor, we rise and we stand,
A family united, in His gentle hand.

Let kindness abound, as rivers do flow,
With every small act, let our spirits glow.
In the tapestry woven of joy and of pain,
Each thread tells a story of love's sweet refrain.

Beneath the vast sky, we find our true home,
In laughter, in tears, no one needs to roam.
Grace fills our cups, until they overflow,
We share what we have, and the love only grows.

As conduits of blessings, we walk hand in hand,
In the garden of faith, together we stand.
With each step we take, let our hearts understand,
We're woven in love, eternally planned.

## Labyrinth of Belief

Within the labyrinth, our spirits entwine,
Searching for truth in the heart's pure design.
The walls may be high, yet hope sees us through,
In shadows of doubt, faith shines ever true.

Every turn we make, a lesson unfolds,
In whispers of wisdom, the divine truth holds.
Though the path may be twisted, the goal is clear,
To find our way home, where love draws us near.

With each step we tread, let compassion guide,
In the maze of existence, we never divide.
Hand in hand we journey, through trials and grace,
For God's loving presence is always our place.

The heart is our compass, the spirit our light,
In the labyrinth's fold, we emerge from the night.
Together we follow the path of our dreams,
For in faith, we discover our true self, it seems.

Though the road may be winding, we shall not stray,
In the labyrinth of belief, we find our way.
Embracing the journey, with love at the helm,
In the sacred maze, our spirits overwhelm.

## The Awakening Journey

In the stillness, whispers call,
Leading souls from shadows tall.
Each step forward, a heart's embrace,
In the journey, find your grace.

Stars above, they guide the way,
Radiant light, they softly play.
With every breath, a promise made,
In the silence, doubts shall fade.

Mountains rise, but faith climbs higher,
In the depths, ignites the fire.
Through storms that threaten to divide,
Love is found, forever tied.

Nature sings a sacred hymn,
In the dark, the light won’t dim.
Across each valley, hope will soar,
In the journey, seek the more.

Hand in hand, our spirits rise,
In the truth, no need for lies.
Awakening, we stand shoulder to shoulder,
With each new dawn, our hearts grow bolder.

## Echoes of the Eternal

In the quiet, listen near,
Echoes whisper, soft and clear.
Timeless stories from days of yore,
Calling hearts to seek the core.

Waves of love in the ocean vast,
Remind us of our sacred past.
With every pulse, a beat divine,
In the unity, hearts align.

Mountaintops, with voices loud,
Echo grace within the crowd.
In the shadows, light will gleam,
In our souls, the ancient dream.

Each moment filled with sacred breath,
In the circle, life from death.
Through the ages, truth will flow,
In the echoes, wisdom grow.

Find the path where silence sings,
In the stillness, spirit wings.
Across the ages, we shall stand,
Bound by love's unconquered hand.

## Beacons of Spiritual Light

From the darkness, candles blaze,
Lighting up the endless maze.
In their glow, we find our way,
Guiding us to brighter days.

Fires of hope in every heart,
Each flicker plays a vital part.
Boundless love, a warm embrace,
In the light, no hidden space.

Through the valleys, shadows creep,
Yet in our souls, the light runs deep.
Each beacon shines against the night,
In the darkness, we ignite.

Hearts aflame with truth's delight,
In the journey, find the height.
With every step, we rise and cheer,
In each witness, love is near.

Together we stand, hand in hand,
Facing fears, we dare to stand.
Beacons bright, our spirits soar,
In the light, forevermore.

**The Blessings of Each New Step**

With each dawn, a blessing comes,
Softly whispered, like the drums.
Every step, a chance to grow,
In the blessings, love will flow.

On this path, where fate will lead,
In the moments, plant the seed.
Through the trials, courage fights,
In the darkness, shine the lights.

Gratitude for every breath,
In the cycle, life and death.
As we tread this sacred land,
In our hearts, we understand.

With faith as our unwavering guide,
Across the broken, there's pride.
Every step, a tale unfolds,
In the journey, courage holds.

Together we rise, ever blessed,
In the journey, we find rest.
With each new step, hearts entwine,
In the blessings, love shall shine.

## Divine Compass

In the quiet morn, a whisper calls,
Guiding hearts beyond the walls.
Faith's light shines in the darkest night,
Mapping souls to purest light.

Hands uplifted, spirits soar,
Each step taken, blessings pour.
With love's embrace, we journey far,
Trusting always our guiding star.

In grace, we find the highest path,
Away from doubt and shadowed wrath.
A compass true, our heart's delight,
Lead us, Lord, through darkest night.

Each prayer a ripple, each wish a stream,
Flowing forth from the sacred dream.
In unity, our spirits rise,
To meet the heavens, to meet the skies.

With every dawn, a promise stands,
In the palm of His loving hands.
Our journey blessed, our purpose clear,
In the heart of faith, we banish fear.

**The Way of Seraphs**

Through realms of light, the seraphs glide,
With wings of love, they gently bide.
In symphonies of grace, they sing,
Of holy love and wondrous spring.

They guard the paths where hearts will tread,
In sacred realms where angels spread.
With wisdom deep, they guide our way,
In every night, in every day.

To dance in joy, to soar in praise,
In the divine light, our spirits raise.
Through trials faced, we find our song,
In the embrace where we belong.

With each soft glow, they light our fears,
In silent prayers, they dry our tears.
A presence felt, a love embraced,
In the arms of light, we are graced.

Together we walk, hand in hand,
In the sacred glow, we take a stand.
With seraphs' wings, our hearts ignite,
In the journey of faith, our souls take flight.

## Guiding Stars

In the velvet skies, the stars do gleam,
Each shining point a holy dream.
They whisper truths from realms above,
A beacon bright of boundless love.

Through trials faced and paths unknown,
Their light will guide us, never alone.
In darkest hours, they hold our sight,
As we walk forth to claim the light.

With faith as strong as the moonlit tide,
We find our way with hearts open wide.
In each twinkling spark, a promise clear,
In every soul, the love we steer.

In unity, we reach for the skies,
With every prayer, our spirit flies.
The stars above, our sisterhood,
In their wise glow, we find the good.

Embrace the light, let shadows fade,
In each guiding star, our hopes are laid.
Together we stand, hearts ever true,
In the celestial dance, we are renewed.

## Sanctified Steps

Each step we take, a holy quest,
In love's embrace, we find our rest.
With every prayer, the journey starts,
In sanctified steps, we seek the heart.

Through valleys deep and mountains high,
We cling to faith, our spirits fly.
With grace as armor, we rise anew,
In sacred light, our purpose true.

With whispered hopes, we chart our course,
In every trial, we find our source.
The gentle call of love divine,
In every heartbeat, His will align.

As rivers run and seasons change,
Our path unfolds, the world re-arranged.
In every moment, His presence near,
In sanctified steps, we cast away fear.

Together we walk, hand in hand,
In the love that forever stands.
With each new dawn, a chance to grow,
In sacred steps, let our faith glow.

## Seasons of Faith

In springtime's bloom, hope takes flight,
Where flowers dance in warm sunlight.
Each bud a prayer, softly spoken,
In faith's embrace, our hearts unbroken.

Through summer's heat, the spirit's glow,
With gathered strength, our kindness show.
The warmth of love in every heart,
In unity, we play our part.

As autumn leaves begin to fall,
We gather wisdom, heed the call.
In gratitude, we share our breath,
Embracing life, we conquer death.

Winter's chill may test our will,
Yet in the stillness, hope can fill.
For in the dark, the stars still shine,
A guiding light, the path divine.

So seasons change, and faith holds fast,
In every trial, love's shadows cast.
With open hearts, we've found our way,
In God's embrace, we choose to stay.

## Whispers of the Divine

In quiet moments, whispers rise,
A sacred song beneath the skies.
In nature's hush, we hear the call,
A gentle touch that cradles all.

The rustling leaves, the flowing stream,
Each breath a note, each glance a dream.
In every heartbeat, love's refrain,
A melody that heals our pain.

Beneath the stars, in moonlit grace,
We seek the truth, we find our place.
In whispered prayers, our souls align,
With every breath, we're truly thine.

In strength and trouble, hope remains,
A guiding force through both joys and pains.
With every struggle, faith will shine,
In every heart, the love divine.

So let us listen, let us hear,
The sacred whispers drawing near.
In quietude, our spirits soar,
Together bound, forevermore.

## Streams of Blessing

From mountain peaks, the rivers flow,
In waters pure, our spirits grow.
Each gentle stream, a gift bestowed,
In blessings rich, our hearts erode.

The sunlight dances on the waves,
In every drop, a love that saves.
We gather hope, in torrents wide,
With open hands, we stand beside.

Beneath the surface, life abounds,
In currents swift, the grace surrounds.
A waterfall of holy grace,
In every wave, we find our place.

As raindrops fall, our souls ignite,
In every storm, the path is bright.
Through trials deep, we find our way,
In streams of faith, our truth will stay.

So let the waters pour and mix,
With every drop, our spirit fix.
In streams of blessing, life will thrive,
In unity, our hearts alive.

**Wings of Transformation**

From caterpillar to butterfly,
With faith in change, we learn to fly.
In sacred winds, our spirits rise,
With open hearts, we touch the skies.

In every struggle, strength is born,
A greater purpose in the morn.
With courage found in trials faced,
We journey forth, our fears erased.

The weight of doubt begins to fade,
With every step, God's love displayed.
In transformation, light appears,
A chorus sung through joyous tears.

As wings unfold, the world we greet,
Each path we walk, a dance of sweet.
In love's embrace, we shed the past,
With grateful hearts, we breathe at last.

So let us rise on wings of grace,
Each flight a step to find our place.
With faith as guide, we can believe,
In transformation, we receive.

## Veils of the Future

In shadows cast by fleeting time,
We seek the light, a path to climb.
With faith our guide, we tread anew,
Unraveling dreams, the world in view.

Each moment holds a sacred grace,
A whispered promise, a warm embrace.
Through trials faced and lessons learned,
The heart ignites, the spirit yearned.

Though veils may hide what lies ahead,
In trust we walk, where angels tread.
The future waits, a canvas bright,
With each step forward, we find the light.

So gather hope, let love expand,
Together woven, hand in hand.
For in the dawn, our souls unite,
Veils lift to show the purest sight.

## Sacred Undertakings

In every prayer, a mission dear,
To lift the lost and dry each tear.
With hearts aflame, we stand as one,
In sacred undertakings begun.

Each sacred word, a seed we sow,
In fields of faith, love's virtue grow.
Compassion's touch, a balm for pain,
In unity, resilience gained.

Through selfless acts, we change the tide,
In humble grace, we do abide.
For in our hands, the power shines,
To heal the world, to break the binds.

So let us rise, at dawn's first glow,
With courage strong, we'll ever sow.
Sacred undertakings weave our fate,
A tapestry of love so great.

**Navigating the Infinite**

In the stillness of the night so deep,
We ponder paths our souls must keep.
Navigating spaces vast and wide,
With faith as compass, we shall abide.

The stars above, like dreams do gleam,
Reflecting hopes, they shine and beam.
Through endless void, our spirits soar,
In cosmic dance, forevermore.

Though trials come, we learn to fly,
With every fall, we touch the sky.
For in the dark, A voice will call,
Guiding us gently, lest we fall.

In harmony with all that is,
We find our purpose, our truest bliss.
Navigating through the endless night,
Our hearts aflame, forever bright.

## Tapestry of Destiny

Threads of fate, a loom divine,
Woven stories, yours and mine.
Each choice a strand, bright colors blend,
In a tapestry where lives extend.

With faith we stitch in joy and strife,
Every moment, a thread of life.
Through joy and pain, our hearts entwine,
Creating beauty, so pure, so fine.

The patterns shift, as seasons change,
Yet love remains, forever strange.
In every heart, a tale unique,
A tapestry of dreams we seek.

So as we walk this sacred art,
Let kindness flow, from heart to heart.
In unity, our lives we blend,
A tapestry of love, no end.

## Horizon of Ancient Promises

In twilight's glow, the ancients call,
Whispers of hope in shadows fall.
Each promise steeped in sacred lore,
Guiding the souls to the eternal shore.

The stars align in sacred dance,
An echo of faith in every glance.
With hearts aflame, our spirits rise,
Together we walk beneath vast skies.

The earth beneath bears witness true,
To the vows we make and the love we woo.
In silence deep, their strength we find,
A tapestry woven, forever entwined.

Rivers of grace flow through the land,
Joining our hearts with a gentle hand.
Each step a promise, divine and bold,
In the book of life, our tales unfold.

So let us stand with open eyes,
As the sun retreats and the spirit flies.
With faith as our anchor, we journey on,
Embracing the light till the break of dawn.

**Navigating Life's Sacred Path**

Each moment filled with grace and light,
We tread upon this path so bright.
With humble hearts and open minds,
In harmony, our spirit binds.

The winds of change will guide our way,
Through trials faced in night and day.
In every choice, a lesson learn,
With gentle hands, to love we turn.

The mountains high, the valleys low,
Wherever we wander, His love will show.
Each step we take, His light ignites,
In the shadows, His presence ignites.

Whispers of faith in every soul,
Connecting hearts, we make them whole.
In service shared, our strength will rise,
To forge a future beneath the skies.

With each sunrise, a chance renewed,
To reflect His grace in all we do.
Together we journey, united as one,
Navigating life's path till the day is done.

## The Celestial Awakening

Awakened by the morning star,
A sacred call from near and far.
The heavens sing a melody pure,
In every heart, His love will cure.

Soft whispers breathe through skies of blue,
Reminding us of all that's true.
With open arms, we celebrate,
The blessings poured, we elevate.

In quiet moments, truth resides,
A steadfast light that never hides.
Each heartbeat echoes wisdom's grace,
Together we join in this embrace.

The moonlit nights reflect our dreams,
With every prayer, His presence beams.
In sacred space, we find our peace,
A journey shared that will never cease.

The stars above, our guiding light,
Illuminating paths through the night.
As we awaken, let's not forget,
The heavens call, we're forever set.

## Dreams at the Edge of Faith

At the edge of faith, our dreams arise,
Lifting spirits toward the skies.
In shadows deep, a spark ignites,
Guiding us through the darkest nights.

With each heartbeat, a hope reborn,
As dawn breaks forth, a new day's sworn.
Together we stand, hands held high,
With dreams of love that never die.

Through valleys low and mountains steep,
In whispered prayers, our promises keep.
A tapestry woven from love's own thread,
In the soil of faith, our dreams are fed.

In every trial, a chance is found,
To build the bridges that hold us bound.
Beyond horizons, we chase the light,
With hearts united, our spirits bright.

So let our dreams take flight today,
At the edge of faith, we choose our way.
In every heartbeat, echoes of grace,
Together we find our sacred space.

## Soulful Quests of Enlightenment

In the stillness of the dawn,
Hearts awaken to the call,
Seeking truths in whispered thoughts,
As shadows cradle all.

Paths of light and hidden grace,
Guide the searching soul,
Through valleys deep and mountains high,
In unity, we become whole.

With every breath, a step we take,
Towards the sacred flame,
Illuminating the darkest fears,
In love, we find our name.

Voices rise in tranquil hymns,
Echoing through the skies,
The journey's goal is not the end,
But the wisdom that around us lies.

In the heart of solitude,
A deeper bond unfolds,
Connecting all in silent grace,
As the ancient truth is told.

## Revelations in Quietude

In moments wrapped in hush,
Where silence speaks profound,
A revelation gently blooms,
In stillness, all is found.

The whispers of the cosmos sing,
Within the soul's embrace,
As questions fade in sacred light,
Time holds us in its grace.

Every heartbeat echoes hope,
In the void, a spark ignites,
Illuminating the path ahead,
With divine guiding lights.

Gratitude like morning dew,
Adorns the tender mind,
In the depth of quietude,
The heart's true voice we find.

And there amidst the tranquil night,
A dance of stars begin,
Revealing mysteries untold,
As we connect within.

## The Sacred Dance of Life's Path

Underneath the moonlit sky,
We tread our sacred ground,
Each footstep marks a promise made,
In the love that we have found.

With every twist of fate we face,
The rhythm guides our way,
And through the storms, the gentle grace,
Turns night to blessed day.

In unity, we rise and fall,
A dance of hearts entwined,
For in each step, we learn to trust,
That life is intertwined.

The sacred dance of joy and grief,
Leads us to higher planes,
Where every tear and laugh we share,
Are threads within love's reign.

So let the music stir our souls,
As we journey hand in hand,
In life’s eternal, sacred dance,
Together, we shall stand.

## Resilient Spirits on the Ascent

With every trial we embrace,
Our spirits rise anew,
Resilient hearts will find their strength,
To push on through the blue.

Amidst the shadows of despair,
A glimmer shines so bright,
Each setback cradles wisdom deep,
In the depth of darkest night.

We soar upon the wings of faith,
As courage lights the flame,
Creating paths where none exist,
And we become the same.

In unity, our voices blend,
A chorus so profound,
Together on this climb we share,
Our purpose tightly bound.

Resilient spirits, onward bound,
With love, our guiding star,
Through every struggle, we ascend,
Together, near and far.

## The Tapestry of the Unseen Path

In the silence, whispers dwell,
Threads of fate, a sacred spell.
Each choice woven, divine design,
Guided by hands, unseen, benign.

Stars align in the velvet night,
Casting dreams, igniting light.
Every step, a pledge we make,
In faith we rise, our fears we shake.

Mountains tall, valleys deep,
Promises made, and secrets keep.
Through trials faced, our spirits soar,
With every heartbeat, we seek more.

Grateful hearts, we walk the line,
In unity, our souls entwine.
Though shadows loom, we shall not stray,
For love will guide us day by day.

In the end, the tapestry bright,
Threads of grace, woven in light.
Together we shall find our way,
In the heart of night, we shall not sway.

## Harmony of Faith's Journey

In the dawn of each new day,
We rise to meet the light's soft sway.
With whispered prayers upon our lips,
We take this path, each heart equipped.

Through storm and calm, we find our peace,
In faith's embrace, our doubts release.
Together we sing a sacred song,
In harmony, we all belong.

Mounting joy on wings of grace,
As we tread this holy space.
With every step, the spirit glows,
In love's embrace, our purpose grows.

Mirrored souls in the sacred dance,
Guided by faith, we take our chance.
In the valleys and on the heights,
We find our way, igniting lights.

With gratitude, we walk as one,
For every trial that we have done.
In the journey of faith, we find
The harmony of heart and mind.

## Footprints on Holy Ground

In the dust, our footprints lie,
Marked by faith beneath the sky.
As we journey, hand in hand,
We bless the earth, this sacred land.

Each step a testament of grace,
In trials faced, we find our place.
With every echo of the past,
We feel the love, forever cast.

In the stillness, whispers call,
Guiding us through every fall.
The heartbeats of the world align,
With purpose clear, our path divine.

Through valleys low, and mountains high,
In every tear, a reason why.
Faith leads on, our guiding sound,
In the footprints left on holy ground.

Together we rise, together we stand,
With steadfast hearts, a faith-command.
Past and future, all entwined,
In the footprints on holy ground, defined.

## Illuminated Shadows of Tomorrow

In twilight's glow, shadows dance,
Secrets whispered, a sacred chance.
With every step, the light grows clear,
Illuminated paths, we draw near.

Beyond the veil, the stars unfold,
Stories of faith and love retold.
With hope as our flame, we reach today,
Into the unknown, we find our way.

The heart's soft murmur, a guiding star,
In darkness deep, we wander far.
Each glimmer seen through trials faced,
In love's embrace, we seek our place.

Fleeting shadows, yet boldly we stand,
With courage forged in love's warm hand.
The journey ahead, though vast and wide,
In faith we trust, our hearts our guide.

For in the light of tomorrow's dawn,
We carry hope, though shadows are drawn.
Together we shine, through thick and thin,
In illuminated shadows, we begin.

## The Tread of Faith

In shadows deep, our hearts align,
With whispers soft, the stars will shine.
Each step we take, a sacred thread,
In trust we walk, where angels tread.

Through trials fierce, our spirits soar,
With faith unbent, we seek for more.
In valleys low, or mountains high,
We find our strength, as time flows by.

The path is lit by sacred grace,
In every heart, a warm embrace.
Through storms and calm, we shall not fear,
For love surrounds, our guide is near.

Each prayer a banner raised on high,
In unity, our voices cry.
With every breath, in peace we stand,
Together strong, hand in hand.

The journey bold, with purpose clear,
In every trial, the light draws near.
In faith we rise, our spirits take flight,
Forever blessed, we walk in light.

## Mirages of Grace

In desert sands, we seek the pure,
With faithful hearts, the soul is sure.
Through wavering sights, we learn to see,
The grace bestowed, eternally.

Amidst the heat, a cool stream flows,
With gentle hands, our spirit grows.
Each moment cherished, love's sweet dance,
In every heartbeat, a sacred chance.

Though shadows play, and doubts may rise,
We find the truth beyond the lies.
In whispered prayers, our hopes take flight,
Guided by faith, we touch the light.

Each step we take, a story told,
In every heart, the fire of gold.
With every breath, we seek the face,
Of love divine, in mirages of grace.

Let not despair eclipse the day,
For in our hearts, light finds its way.
Together we walk through joy and pain,
In fields of grace, our souls remain.

## Pathways to the Divine

In silence deep, the spirit wakes,
Amidst the noise, the stillness quakes.
Each thought a seed, in soil of prayer,
We nurture faith with utmost care.

Through winding roads, our feet shall roam,
Each step a note, in heaven's poem.
In every heart, a longing grows,
To find the source, where love bestows.

With every dawn, the sun shall rise,
Illuminating all our sighs.
In trust we tread, with purpose clear,
In every heartbeat, God is near.

Through valleys low, and mountains steep,
The promise made, our souls to keep.
With open hearts, we journey on,
Through paths of light, we greet the dawn.

Together strong, we walk as one,
In unity, our will be done.
For every path that we pursue,
Leads ever closer to the true.

## Journey of Faith Unfolding

In gentle steps, the journey starts,
With every beat, we share our hearts.
The road ahead, uncharted lands,
In faith we trust, with willing hands.

Through trials faced, the fire refines,
In every storm, a peace entwines.
For lessons learned, in pain and grace,
We find our way, through time and space.

With every prayer, the spirit sings,
In unity, our hope takes wings.
Through shadows cast, and light that breaks,
We rise in joy, for love awakes.

The journey long, yet never lone,
In every heart, a place called home.
With courage bold, we seek the call,
In faith we stand, together fall.

The path unfolds, with each sunrise,
In every tear, the promise lies.
With hearts aglow, we face the day,
In journey's grace, forever stay.

## Footprints of Reverence

In the quiet of the dawn's soft glow,
I wander where the sacred waters flow.
Whispers of the ancients, gently call,
In the stillness, I find the heart of all.

Each step a prayer upon the earth,
A journey marked by humble mirth.
I trace the paths where saints have tread,
Finding peace in the words they've said.

Beneath the arches of the olden trees,
I listen to the songs upon the breeze.
Echoes of love in the rustling leaves,
A tapestry of wonder that believes.

With open arms, the skies stretch wide,
In every shadow, the Light does abide.
Footprints left by those who dared to dream,
In their embrace, my spirit finds its beam.

Through valleys deep and mountains high,
Faith leads me onward, I cannot deny.
For in each moment, a holy trace,
In the journey of time, I find my place.

## Embrace of the Unknown

Beyond the horizon where the day meets night,
I stand in silence, wrapped in twilight.
The stars awaken, a tender show,
In the embrace of the unknown, I grow.

Each question lingers, a sacred thread,
Binding my heart to what lies ahead.
In the stillness, whispers softly play,
Guiding the spirit on its destined way.

With every heartbeat, faith ignites,
Illuminating shadows, casting lights.
The mystery around me, vast and wide,
Beckons a trust I can no longer hide.

In the depths of doubt, a spark remains,
Hope like a river courses through my veins.
I welcome the unknown with arms outstretched,
For in its depths, my soul is etched.

And as the dawn breaks, a promise unfolds,
Each day a story, a truth to behold.
In the unknown lies a sacred trust,
I embrace the journey, in Him, I must.

## Celestial Pathways

Beneath the arch of heavens wide,
Celestial pathways, where spirits bide.
Guiding the wanderers, starlit grace,
In the dance of light, I find my place.

With every breath, I feel the sky,
Whispers of angels, as they fly.
In the heavens' heart, I lay my fears,
A symphony of love, for all the years.

The moon and sun in eternal dance,
Invite the heart to take a chance.
For in the cosmos, a truth abounds,
In every heartbeat, the divine resounds.

Milestones of hope, marked by the stars,
Lessons of love, written in scars.
On this celestial journey, I rise and roam,
In the embrace of sky, I find my home.

As the universe spins, I trust the flow,
Each heartbeat a testament, a holy glow.
In celestial pathways, my spirit soars,
With faith as my guide, forever explores.

## Faith's Unseen Way

On faith's unseen path, I tread so light,
Guided by whispers that dance out of sight.
In the shadowed valleys where doubts may dwell,
I carry the spark of a promise to tell.

Through murky waters and stormy skies,
I seek the truth that forever lies.
With each step forward, the courage grows,
Wrapped in the stillness, God's love flows.

In moments of chaos, I find my peace,
A gentle reminder that fears release.
Though unseen are the hands that guide,
In heart's deep chambers, I confide.

With faith as my anchor, I journey wide,
In the arms of the Spirit, I gladly abide.
For though the road may twist and turn,
In the silence of faith, my heart will discern.

As dawn unveils the morning sun,
I stand in wonder, the race is won.
In faith's unseen way, I walk each day,
For in every step, I know He'll stay.

## Seraphic Bliss in Transition

In the radiance of light, we soar,
Guided by angels, we seek the shore.
Heaven whispers sweetly, in divine grace,
We move with courage, in love's embrace.

Amidst the shadows, our spirits unite,
Stars lead the way through the velvet night.
In every heartbeat, the sacred resounds,
In moments of silence, true peace abounds.

Each step a promise, each breath a prayer,
Together we journey, with hope laid bare.
Through trials we strengthen, through fears we mend,
In the arms of the holy, we find our end.

Faith is the anchor, steadfast and sure,
In love's gentle hands, we find the cure.
Transcending the turmoil, we rise above,
In this seraphic dance, we're cradled in love.

So onward we glide, on wings made of light,
With hearts intertwined, we embrace the night.
Seraphic bliss awaits in the dawn,
A promise of peace, in our journey drawn.

**Revelations in the Dust of the Journey**

In the dust of the road, truths emerge,
Whispers of wisdom, our souls to urge.
Through trials and burdens, the spirit reveals,
In each heavy step, a heart that heals.

Footprints of prophets, in shadows and sun,
Guiding the seekers till the race is run.
In every struggle, a lesson bestowed,
Each bend in the path, a new seed sowed.

When thorns prick the flesh, and tears stain the ground,
Hope is the echo, in silence profound.
For every sorrow, a blossom takes flight,
In darkness, a promise of radiant light.

As we walk the terrain of the weary and worn,
We carry the light, though our spirits may mourn.
With reverent hearts, we embrace the vast,
In revelations found, deep shadows are cast.

So gather the moment, let love be the guide,
In the dust of the journey, the truth will abide.
Through faith, we arise, united and bold,
In every story shared, the divine unfolds.

## Prayerful Steps into the Unknown

With every soft step, in shadows we tread,
Whispering prayers, the spirit is fed.
The path is uncertain, yet faith lights the way,
In the stillness of night, our fears fade away.

Hearts full of wonder, we reach for the sky,
In the depths of silence, we learn how to fly.
Guided by love, through the trials we face,
Each moment unfolds, wrapped in grace.

The winds of the world, they murmur and sway,
Yet onward we journey, come what may.
In the unknown's embrace, we find our peace,
Every step taken, sweet burdens release.

Faith’s gentle whisper, our compass, our chart,
In prayerful resolve, we open our heart.
With each new horizon, the spirit ignites,
In prayerful steps forward, the soul takes flight.

So venture with courage, though pathways may twist,
In the journey of life, we hold tight to bliss.
Our hearts are the vessels, our spirits the flame,
In prayerful steps forward, we grow, never tame.

## Visioning a Future with Faith

In the dawn of creation, we dream and aspire,
Visioning futures, we reach for the fire.
With hearts full of hope and eyes set above,
We gather our dreams like the stars, all in love.

Each story woven, with threads divine,
In the fabric of hope, we see the design.
Though challenges rise like storms in the night,
With faith as our anchor, we stand in the light.

Together we build on the foundation laid,
With courage ignited, our fears allayed.
In the dance of creation, we joyfully spin,
A symphony rising, where dreams can begin.

The future is bright, with a promise in sight,
In the warmth of connection, we find our light.
In each loving gesture, in life's sacred flow,
Visioning futures, together we grow.

So lift up your eyes, let your spirit take flight,
In the vision of faith, we illuminate night.
With love as our lantern, and hope as our guide,
We journey together, with hearts open wide.

Milton Keynes UK
Ingram Content Group UK Ltd.
UKHW031320271124
451618UK00007B/195

9 789916 896884